DREAD

BOOKS BY AI

DREAD

Ai

W. W. Norton & Company
New York London

For information about permission to reproduce selections from this book,
write to Permissions, W. W. Norton & Company, Inc., 500 Fifth Avenue,
New York, NY 10110

Manufacturing by Courier Westford
Book design by Blue Shoe Studio
Production manager: Julia Druskin

Library of Congress Cataloging-in-Publication Data

Ai, 1947–
    Dread / by Ai.—1st ed.
        p.   cm.
    ISBN 0-393-04143-3 (hardcover)
    1. Title.
    PS3551.I2 D74 2003
    811'.54—dc21   2002153050

W. W. Norton & Company, Inc.
500 Fifth Avenue, New York, N.Y. 10110
www.wwnorton.com

W. W. Norton & Company Ltd.
Castle House, 75/76 Wells Street London W1T 3QT

1 2 3 4 5 6 7 8 9 0

THIS BOOK IS DEDICATED
TO THE SURVIVORS OF CHILDHOOD TRAUMA
AND TO GWENDOLYN BROOKS

CONTENTS

THE POEMS IN THIS BOOK HAVE APPEARED
IN THE FOLLOWING MAGAZINES AND ANTHOLOGIES:

Callaloo: "The Greenwood Cycle," "The White Homegirl";
Canary River: "Dread"; *Columbia Magazine*: "Rude
Awakening"; *Crazy Horse*: "Intercourse,"
"The Psychic Detective: Identity"; *Divide*: "Greetings
Friend"; *Estrella Mountain Community College*:
"Family"; *Etruscan Press*: "Fairy Tale"; *The Manthology*:
"The Broker," "The Calling"; *New Delta Review*: "The
Secret"; *Pacific Review*: "Lullaby," "Grandfather Says";
Southeast Review: "Delusion"; *Witness*: "The Psychic
Detective: Fantasy"; *The Writer's Garret*: "Passage"

DREAD

DREAD

My name is Shirley Herlihy,
but to the lowlifes on my beat,
I am Officer Girlie.
They do not mean to diss me.
It is a sign of respect
that I let them think is ok with me, and it is,
when I am trying to do my community policing.
After my brother disappeared
at the World Trade Center,
the word went out.
The lowlifes even gave me a bouquet of flowers
I could not accept.
They came from the Korean store
before somebody tossed a Molotov cocktail
through the front door
in retaliation for a "situation"
that involved the girlfriend of a drug dealer
shoplifting disposable diapers and Tampax.
The fact is I appreciated the thought
if not the deed.
I mean the flowers were at least a sign
I had not become a cop
turning a blind eye on the misery of the street.
I was known as someone who was tough,
but fair in meting out justice.

God knows it's hard to toe the line
every single time a perp messes up, but I tried.
If somebody's mother needed a ride
to a bail hearing,
my transportation specialist,
Bobby J, the gypsy cab guy would oblige.
I'd say thanks by slipping him
tickets to a ball game, a movie
or some lame excuse for entertainment.
I kept the wheels turning,
so I didn't fall under them.
I only had to use my gun once in two years
against a sonofabitch
who murdered his uncle
and hid his body in a dumpster.
Original, huh?
Stanko, the wino, found him on his garbage rounds.
We cornered the asshole in an alley
behind that shooting gallery
in the building that's now been gentrified
and is home to a decorater, six cats
and stacks of old cool jazz albums.
Anyway, the asshole said he had nothing to lose
fired and missed, fired again
and clipped me in the shins,
but I got him as I went down.
He died, but the paramedics revived him
and now he's in prison.
He's born again and keeps claiming Christ has risen,
as if nobody heard the news.
Once in a while, he calls me to apologize

and proselytize. I let him last time,
even as I sat, holding the telephone,
wishing my brother would come back.
I keep telling myself he's gone forever,
but it's so hard to accept.
He was always rescuing things
when we were kids—injured cats, birds,
even a German shepherd
who had been known to bite without provocation.
I used to tease him by singing,
"Patrick Kevin's going to Heaven."
I wonder if he made it,
or if he's suspended between the life
that didn't mean much to him
and the death that means everything to me?
He was such a good boy.
He would have been a better man, if only . . .
After our parents died
when I was fifteen going on twenty-five
and he was twelve, we raised ourselves.
No one else had the time.
It's a busy world out there
the addicts tell me and I believe them
because I know.
I bet they're lining up at Smitty's
crack house right now to score.
I should be there to arrest someone,
but I've turned in my badge and gun
and come downtown to search this crater
for some sign of Pat,
even if it's only a feeling

that he's still around in spirit at least,
if not in body.
There're just a few of us
who won't give up.
With our shovels, picks and garden tools
we dig among the hunks of steel,
the concrete and remnants of people
who went to work one day
and vanished into our memories.
I dread finding him and dread I won't
as I choke from the fumes less poisonous
than the hope that keeps me awake at night,
but I can't give up.
He'd do the same for me.
Patrick Kevin Herlihy, I repeat under my breath
as I uncover another credit card
and a wallet with something that looks
suspiciously like blackened flesh fused to it.
I turn them in and return to digging
until faint from the effort and fumes, I collapse.
Two other searchers take me by each arm
and help me to a chair,
but I don't stay there long.
After a candy bar and a glass of water,
I'm back at my task.
On the job, I never questioned what I was.
I had my role to play
in the day to day give
and mostly take of the criminals
who inhabited my world,
but this sixty acres is a city of ghosts

and I don't know where I stand with them.
When I arrived this morning,
nothing greeted me but the wind
and a grackle making a din
as it pecked and scratched
at flat, charred patches of ground.
Maybe it's a good sign
that the birds have returned,
a sign of rebirth. But whose? I wonder,
as I stare at my bruised hands.
Last year, I solved the robbery
of a palm reader.
As a lark, I let her read my lines.
She said, "In the future,
you'll find the one you lost,
but it will cost you."
Now as I stand above a hole seventy feet deep,
looking down, I don't see Pat.
When I call his name,
my voice is swallowed up by the roar of machines.
At first, that sound signified the possibility
of finding him
and made my heart beat faster,
but now it's just the white noise
I hear in my nightmares
that always begins at the scene of a shooting
that occurred during a domestic disturbance
between a man and a woman in Queens
that left two teens bereft of a mother and father
and made them cling to one another much too tightly,
so that now the one left behind is frightened

by her utter loneliness
and drinks Irish whiskey at the pub
where her brother, Pat, used to hold up the bar,
promising the patrons he was going to quit drinking
one of these days
and to assorted laughter
call for another round of drinks,
knowing his sister would never let him
sink as low as he wanted to go.
He'd seen the fight. I hadn't
but I was haunted too
although I tried not to show it,
especially to him.
That day when I got home
from basketball practice,
I found Pat cowering under the stairway
as I had so many times before
when our parents fought,
but this time, I knew something was different.
He wasn't crying for a change.
"Are Mom and Dad fighting again?" I asked.
"They were," he said, without a trace of emotion,
then he told me Dad had come into his room,
hugged him and said goodbye.
That's when I knew something terrible had happened.
All the years since, I'd nursed him
through the rough times, the blue funks
and the highs that were too much
and always ended in a rush
of promises to stop drinking.
He worked construction, he'd say,

I wouldn't catch him falling off some scaffolding
high above Manhattan,
even drunk he could maintain his balance.
The truth was he was often unemployed,
but I supported him.
I'd long since moved into our parents' room,
but he stayed in his
across the hall from where they'd died,
surrounded by all his trophies from high school, comics
and posters taped and retaped to the walls.
The week before the attack,
he'd told me he was going back to work.
He'd stopped drinking for good
and I believed him, as I looked deeply into his eyes,
and saw a boy who having barely escaped
the inferno of family violence
would still finally perish in fire's cold embrace.

DELUSION

I watched the Trade Center Towers
burning, then collapse
repeatedly on television,
until I could see them clearly
when I shut my eyes.
The blackened skies even blotted out my vision,
until I screamed and threw myself on the floor
and rolled there as if I were on fire.
That's when I decided to go and claim
my sister's body.
The doctor said I had suffered a psychotic break
and in my delusional state,
it didn't matter that she wasn't there.
I carried a photograph of two women laughing,
one of whom was me, the other a stranger
I met on the street, but I pretended she was my sister.
It became my passport into the suffering of others.
I never took money, only sympathy.
I tried to repay everyone
by serving coffee to the firemen and police.
We shared our sorrow,
ate it like bread.
It was our defense
against the senselessness of it all.
They "wanted" to believe that I was seeking

someone I'd lost
and I absorbed their need.
I understood the power of belief and used it.
My phantom sister gave me the power to deceive.
Since I didn't know what was real anymore,
sometimes I thought I'd died
and was a ghost come back to haunt myself.
I'd catch a glimpse of someone familiar
in the mirror before she disappeared
beneath my face.
Was I a mask the past had taken on,
or some magician's trick gone wrong?
Maybe instead of being sawed in half,
I'd been sawed down the middle
and to the gasps of the audience
part of me had run in one direction
and part in the other.
I searched for my sister,
until at last, the looks of pity and concern
I'd learned to accept without question
made me yearn for escape,
so one day, I packed my suitcase
and faded into the landscape
where it all came back to me.
When I was twelve and my sister was ten,
she drowned in Cape Cod Bay.
At first, we swam side by side
in water so calm and blue
it was almost too beautiful.
When suddenly she sank beneath the waves,
I tried to save her, I really did,

but I couldn't stay underwater long enough.
I could have blamed myself
for I had coaxed her
into swimming so far out when she grew tired,
we couldn't reach shore easily,
but I didn't, I was almost relieved.
She was my parents' favorite
and she annoyed me endlessly.
She would have pulled me under, wouldn't she?
I had to save myself.
At first, I didn't even miss her,
oh it hurt, but like a blister
when you burst it,
then it heals and you forget how it felt,
but I began to dream about her.
Sometimes she cried,
but mostly she claimed she hadn't died at all,
but was simply lost
and finally, I thought I found her
when the Twin Towers came down.

At nineteen, I dropped out of college,
left my family and roamed from city to city.
Sometimes, I took my sister's name.
I played a game with myself.
Who am I today? I'd say, staring into the mirror.
Sometimes like a vampire,
I cast no reflection.
Other times, all I saw
was my wild desire to bring her back.
I was tired all the time.

I quit, or was fired from job after job.
Finally, I asked my parents to send money,
which I used to buy green contact lenses
and breast implants.
I dyed my blonde hair red
and adopted a brogue.
I learned to step dance
and joined an Irish troupe and went on the road.
I did what I fantasized my sister would do.
My mind flew everywhere like a bird on a dare.
I resolved to remain in flight,
but one night, during a performance
my feet simply would not move.
I had to be carried offstage
and lifted into an ambulance.
In the hospital, I chanced to see
the horrible events of September 11th on TV.
The day of my release, I told a nurse,
"I'm well, you know,"
and she didn't even glance my way,
as she replied, "That's what they all say."
On the way to my apartment,
my sister came out of hiding.
"You'll find me at ground zero," she whispered
and I answered, "I know."
"I had a conversation with the dead.
It was all in my head," I said aloud.
No one paid any notice.
I was just another person "with issues"
and on that day in particular
attention was focused elsewhere.

So when I showed up at the lodging
for relatives of survivors,
I had an identity at last
that combined the past with the present.
Still, I couldn't find my sister.
I wondered if she had vaporized,
or whether her body, or part of it
was fused to some piece of metal
I would never see, much less feel.
Maybe she was sealed in a room
beneath tons of debris, I told myself,
then I thought I heard her calling my name
over the cacaphony of machines,
the voices of rescue workers,
and dogs barking
when they caught the scent of a body,
only to discover another body part
and slink off dejectedly,
until at last, even they lost heart.
By then, I didn't have to pretend
I hadn't given up myself,
and given in to the grim truth
unfolding before my eyes.
I came to hate the lie of my sister
even as I became a symbol of sisterly devotion.
I knew I wasn't worthy,
yet, I couldn't stop the forward motion,
propelling me toward the ocean
where she drowned
in glass, metal, fire and ash.
When I couldn't stand it anymore,

I said I got word she'd never been there afterall.
I had received a mysterious telephone call
informing me she'd left her job
at The World Trade Center months ago,
but didn't know how to reach me.
A friend had seen her photo on a kiosk
with my contact number on it
and had gotten in touch with her.
Now she was calling to tell me
to come to her immediately,
so I packed and set out,
but after a few weeks in Atlantic City,
I felt irresistibly drawn back.
I rejoined the search,
until someone remembered me from before,
pausing, unable to allow that I had somehow
fooled him and asked why I had done it.
I'd run out of lies by then
and the energy it takes to keep
those multicolored balls spinning in the air.
I only wanted to be somewhere the grief of others
was as overwhelming as my own.
He didn't understand,
so once again I made a narrow escape,
and found my sister waiting on the Red Line in Boston.
She hugged me, saying,
"We should come here more often,
just the two of us"
and I agreed, easing into the seat beside her.
"There's seaweed in your hair," I said
and she replied, "I don't care. I'm dead."

Then she laid her head against my shoulder.
It was so hot, my blouse burst into flame,
I told her I wouldn't let her down, I'd hold her,
but like all the other times, I let her go.
At the next stop, I got out,
but instead of walking upstairs
and taking Amtrak to New York City,
I stepped into the path of an oncoming train,
because I preferred to stay in the underworld,
with all the other missing boys and girls.

FAIRY TALE

The first time I heard the story
of Red Riding Hood,
I was so afraid of the wolf
I dreamed he ate me for dinner.
The next morning,
mother found bite marks on my arms.
Even though I swore they weren't my teeth,
she punished me for lying
by tying me to a chair,
facing the object of my dread—
a woodcut of the wolf in Grandma's bed,
but I knew it wouldn't make a difference
because the wolf had chosen me.
At twelve, I turned to model airplanes
and my dreams became a means of escape.
High above my body, looking down,
I'd find the wolf in my bed,
as if he too had been released
from some nightmare
and finally could sleep.
Eventually, I dreamed of girls,
but even so, my nocturnal emissions
often ended in visions of the wolf
dressed in women's clothes
whispering my name seductively.

I came to him every time he came to me
just like the kamikaze did in nineteen forty-three,
when the United States was at war with Japan
and I was a pilot.
For some reason, neither of us fired at first.
We just flew side by side,
staring at each other
across the great military divide.
He wasn't wearing goggles
and I swear I could see his eyes
gleaming like black opals
and the expression on his face
was the one the wolf wore
the first time he tasted me.
I think we Catholics call that look transfiguration.
I don't remember how long our strange communion lasted
before I fired on the bastard.
I flew through the smoke and flames
of his disintegration sure that his death
had left me changed and whole,
but today, when borders and oceans
can be crossed as easily as tossing a coin,
as I am on my way to San Xavier Mission,
suddenly, I hear an explosion,
while all around me, the desert steams
under an empty turquoise sky
and once again, I feel as if I am a fragment of myself.
The highway stretches forward and back without traffic.
I am alone, yet I know the wolf's returned to haunt me
as I stop the car by the side of the road.
When I close my eyes,

I remember watching with horror and relief
as the kamikaze's burning body
shot from the wreckage of the plane
and dropped into the ocean below.
I made it home in one piece,
at least on the outside.
Now I'm retired, in good health,
relocated to Tucson, Arizona, from Baltimore
and I've returned to the Church
after forty years of drifting between the New Age
and whatever "this" is.
I breathe deeply, open my eyes and start the car.
I drive the few miles to the Mission,
where I learn of a terrorist attack on New York City.
I ask Father Anthony if what I experienced earlier
was a premonition,
but he says, "My son, I don't know."
"A miracle then," I ask.
"Only if you pass certain tests.
You didn't save anyone, did you?
But if you saw the Virgin, or a saint . . ."
"Only a wolf," I answer, "and a dead man."
"Was the dead man a good man?"
"Maybe once upon a time."
"So was Adam before the Fall," he says.
"Perhaps it was Satan you saw, for this is his work."
"Yes, Father," I say, but I don't believe that either.
The kamikaze was only a man
and the wolf, I must admit at last, is me.
"You aren't the wolf," he says mysteriously . . .
"I'm not?"

"Don't you remember I absolved you of all that?"
"No, I'm getting old," I answer.
"So are we all, but some of us moreso.
You know the wolf is not necessarily evil.
To some Indian people it is a protector spirit."
"But what could the wolf protect me from?"
"Yourself?"
"I'm not convinced of that," I say.
"Then come have coffee," he says.
"We can chat about this latest manmade disaster
and wait for the Second Coming with bated breath."
"You are so eloquent, Father,
but I'm not in the mood for conversation."
"I'll just pray, until I run out of words,
then I'll howl."
"Have you noticed the absence of birdsong?
It's as if they know of the tragedy.
All right, all right I'll go."
"You know the way," he adds,
laying a hairy hand on mine
and I glimpse behind his benign gaze
the face I know so well.
The reports say people jumped to certain death
when the jets rammed into the Twin Towers.
Rather than let death come to them,
they went to him,
their clothes billowing in the wind,
making them look like the kamikaze
in a fiery tailspin.
I kneel, staring at the altar,
trying to connect the dots of my life

that she'd never be unfaithful,
but see how hard promises are to keep, she said,
shouldn't we let sleeping dogs lie?
I'm one big lie, I thought
and she said, "I did it for your own good."
I said, "You should quit while you're ahead
and admit you were ashamed,"
and she said, "That's not true,"
but I knew it was.
Even today, I'm a stranger to her.
When she looks at me, she sees him,
hears him ask her if she's cold
in her thin, wool cardigan, cowboy shirt
loafers and Levis,
her long hair done up in Shirley Temple curls.
He smiles because she's too old
for that hairstyle,
although she's still a girl.
He asks, "Are you lost?
She answers boldly, "Not now."
He was Japanese. He was studying physics
like Albert Einstein, he told her.
When I look in the mirror
sometimes I think I can see his face
imposed over mine,
although it's only an outline really
with a bare fact, a detail
my mother doled out grudgingly.
I truly only see what he left
going faster than any $E=mc^2$ formula

and not getting anywhere,
as mother looks at me with a wolfish grin
and pinches my cheek,
encouraging me to repeat with her,
"The end."

RELATIVITY

Mama says she was lost,
says she asked directions from my father
and doesn't know how they ended up in bed,
or how they created a baby from one afternoon,
a chance meeting at a streetcar stop
in the Japanese neighborhood of Denver.
She was married.
When she told him she was pregnant with his child,
he said, "Go home to your family."
The rest is history, is my story
and I don't know how it ends,
but I hope it's painless when it does,
unlike the end of their affair
which left her gasping for air
as he boarded the streetcar home
to his family and a deep sleep
untroubled by dreams of souls to keep,
but my mother was another story,
Catholic, seventeen and married,
abandoned by the man
she describes as being kind to her,
but how kind could he have been
when he left her to fend for herself,
left her at the top of the stairs,

where she calculated that a fall
might end it all
and sent herself tumbling down them,
only to realize when she came to at the hospital
that she had survived and so had the baby
that was growing inside her
like the truth she could not hide.
When she confessed to her husband, he beat her.
While he was out drinking,
she called her mother and father in Tucson.
They sent her uncle Bill
to take her back home.
She says Uncle and she rode the bus,
not talking until they were out of Colorado.
Uncle had cried when he saw her.
He was that way, you know.
He didn't like women, they said,
he was one of those men,
but they didn't hold that against him
so he was dispatched
to bring my mother and her bastard back.
The family decided that they could hide it all
by allowing everyone to think
I was the husband's daughter.
They didn't worry about the future,
or what that lie might mean to me.
On my birth certificate,
it says he's my father,
but I always knew he wasn't.
The two times I saw him,

I realized my mother was lying,
knew I was the daughter of another,
but I was afraid to ask her about it
and get to the bottom of those stairs
where wracked with guilt and despair,
she finally owned up to her "sin."
She'd never do that again, she tells me,
at least I think that's how she put it
when she told me the truth
or the version of it she'd decided to share.
She says it as if she's talking about someone
she only dimly recognizes
as if I was only a detour on the way
to her real life
and that's what I can't reconcile.
When she said she was just a stupid girl
I thought about how much it had cost her and me,
but I couldn't escape the feeling of displacement
of reeling from the shock of recognition
that doesn't come from finding out
who you really are,
but who you are not,
neither a love child, nor a hate child,
just something that happened
while she wasn't looking.
Her husband was twenty years older.
He ignored her, she said.
He had a girlfriend on the side.
She'd seen them together
and she'd promised herself

that she'd never be unfaithful,
but see how hard promises are to keep, she said,
shouldn't we let sleeping dogs lie?
I'm one big lie, I thought
and she said, "I did it for your own good."
I said, "You should quit while you're ahead
and admit you were ashamed,"
and she said, "That's not true,"
but I knew it was.
Even today, I'm a stranger to her.
When she looks at me, she sees him,
hears him ask her if she's cold
in her thin, wool cardigan, cowboy shirt
loafers and Levis,
her long hair done up in Shirley Temple curls.
He smiles because she's too old
for that hairstyle,
although she's still a girl.
He asks, "Are you lost?
She answers boldly, "Not now."
He was Japanese. He was studying physics
like Albert Einstein, he told her.
When I look in the mirror
sometimes I think I can see his face
imposed over mine,
although it's only an outline really
with a bare fact, a detail
my mother doled out grudgingly.
I truly only see what he left
going faster than any $E=mc^2$ formula

could take him,
escaping fatherhood like any other man
who hadn't planned on staying long,
my otōsan, traveling light,
traveling at the velocity of darkness.

FAMILY

The old man sent for Papa,
but he wouldn't go.
That's what they tell me.
I don't know.
He had land to give him.
He was on his death bed,
but Papa wouldn't go.
Papa said, "Die like a dog, Old Man."
He said it in the shed
where he kept the horse tack.
He said it when he fed the horses.
He said it in bed like a prayer,
then he kissed the only picture
he had of his mother, fell asleep
and woke up another day
and they sent word again.
The Old Man was calling out for him,
but Papa said, "I got a hen's neck to wring.
We're having baked chicken for dinner,"
and he went in the barn
and came out with eggs still warm from laying
and he took them in the kitchen
washed off the shit, put them in a basket
and went to sit on the front porch.
He rocked back and forth in his glider

and Mama brought him a glass of hot apple cider.
"Where's that chicken, John?
Nevermind, I'll do it myself," she said.
"The way he treated my mother," said Papa.
He remembered riding to Texas in a wagon
from Oklahoma when he was five
with his Choctaw mother
and his white father.
An older brother left behind,
because he resembled Choctaws more than Papa did.
"That," he went on, "was a time."
The Old Man on a bay horse,
just staring at him,
until Papa waved,
then turning and riding off.
His father, Charles's silence at dinner,
biscuits and a basket of fried chicken
sent from the ranch house
and a teddy bear with all its fur nearly gone.
"That was mine," said his father,
"now it's yours."
Papa nodded and picked up a chicken leg.
He ate ranch beans, potato salad
and washed it down with buttermilk.
Then his mother put him to bed.
Her long black braid had come undone
and he touched her hair
and it made a sound like silk rustling
in his dreams anyway.
The next day, his father took him to see cattle grazing
as far as the eye could see and further.

He saw a pond for fishing, horses and a bunkhouse,
a doghouse, an outhouse his father once used
and he met a lot of people—cowboys, two cooks
a man who took him up in the saddle of his horse.
That was his uncle, but he didn't know it then.
He died in the Great War.
He didn't see his grandfather.
His father took him in the kitchen of the ranch house.
"You be quiet as a little mouse," he told him.
The cook gave him hot chocolate and a book about the ABC's.
When his father came back, he just said, "Let's go, son."
He didn't return to that house,
until he was twenty,
after his father got killed when a steer trampled him
and ran clear to Abiline,
before anybody could catch it,
at least that's what they say.
Papa didn't know what would happen,
so he started packing.
Then a message came from The Old Man,
whose name was never uttered in their house.
John went that time.
He didn't know what he expected to find.
I'll tell you what he didn't, The Old Man.
The foreman had a letter for him.
It said, "I need a good drover."
He talked it over with his mother,
but she was ready to go back to her people,
so he took her home to Oklahoma,
where he met his brother
and Mama and went back to Texas

with his new bride, a job
and a life this side of respectable.
And so they lived that way for fifteen years.
Grandson and grandfather,
who couldn't put asunder the divisions of race.
Papa gets up. He walks to the gate,
opens it and just waits
for God knows what,
then he steps back and shuts it.
He remembers again the Christmas presents
sent from the ranch house,
always one for him, nothing for his mother
and smothers the urge to kick in the door
of the ranch house
pour gasoline on the Old Man, light it
and watch him burn to a cinder
with a smile on his face.
The same kind The Old Man wore
the day they first came face to face
and The Old Man rode off.
It had no love in it, it had no hate,
but it had kinship.

THE SAGA OF CHARLIE SMITH

For my great-great-grandfather

I had my first Choctaw woman when I was seventeen,
got tired of her, got me another.
I wasn't like my father, who settled for one wife,
and like him, she was Scotch Irish.
They were Catholic, but in desperation,
they had me baptized
by a hellfire and damnation preacher who evangelized
but I wouldn't break my pact with the Devil
who made my desire for red women
such a raging fire.
They almost died when their boat capsized
on the Red River.
They were going to Texas to get away from the Indians and me.
I wouldn't leave, nosiree.
I was born in Choctaw County, Oklahoma.
Back then, it was Indian Territory.
That's what counts in this story.
In those days, you lived the Indian way.
It was easier if you made peace
with the red man, give him a hand
when he needed it and he'd give you one.
You took a wife, raised a bunch of half-breeds.
Nobody made much of it,
unless you made somebody mad

and things got said,
things that could leave you dead,
but by and large, you worked the land
and tried to live like a Christian.
Sounds simple, don't it?—
a few rules to follow
before you got dropped into the ground,
but my second Choctaw wife
wouldn't do nothing I said.
Had to hit her sometimes, hit her in the head,
so she'd understand
what I was trying to teach her.
Nickname was Annie.
She had an Indian name I can't remember,
but I do remember how she would sit on my lap
and bounce up and down on it. What a girl,
but she was wild.
Packed up her rags one day and left me.
I come in from checking on the cattle,
stove was cold, nothing left for Charlie to do
but make bacon and eggs,
twice in one day, mind you.
Soon enough, I got word where she was,
loaded my six-shooter and went to get her.
I found her with a Freedman.
That's what they called freed black slaves
I said, "Come on out, you black sumbitch.
I'm itching to kill you."
He come out shooting, all the while
she was crying.
Meanwhile, I was shot through my thigh,

blood running into my boot kinda tickled me
and hurt too, of course.
I musta blacked out, because when I came to,
she run at me with a knife, screaming,
"You killed my daddy."
Well, I just about soiled my pants.
She had never said a word to me about a daddy.
I thought she didn't have one.
She didn't even look like one athem mixtures,
looked full-blooded to me,
but maybe I just couldn't see it, being a white man
and not used to how they turn out.
I mean, I had seen some of them.
They looked like any other coloreds to me.
"I'll be," I said, then out come her uncle.
I knew him. He was part white.
"What the hell?" I told him, "This is too confusing.
A man ought to know who he's shooting, oughtn't he?"
He raised holy hell about it, then whispered, "Good shooting,"
to me under his breath.
I just wanted my wife to come back.
She did a few days after the funeral,
caught me in bed with the redheaded daughter
of that Irish pots and pans mender,
who used her to get work.
She knew how to make a man feel like a man
if you know what I mean,
not like my first wife, Iola, who lay there
wincing the whole time.
Annie cursed me in Choctaw. I knew what she said,
but I kept it to myself.

The redhead cried, "You going to let that squaw
talk to you that way?
She says she's going to cut it off."
"Why Moira, I didn't know you could speak Choctaw," I said
like it was just an ordinary observation,
as she dressed
and left me trying to defend myself.
A few days later, the tribal police come to my place.
They asked me to ride with them in a friendly way,
but I knew they wasn't.
They was relatives of Annie's.
I told them I'd come after I fed the cattle,
then saddled up and rode hard into Texas.
That ride made me a fugitive from justice,
but Indians don't mess with white men in Texas,
so I became what I had always been,
a white man who had lived among Indians,
but had not become one of them.
I had tried. I'd married their women
would have had children then too,
but the first one, a bastard, was stillborn
and my fourth, or fifth wife, a Cherokee, got rid of one
by using some remedy her mother brought with her
when she walked the Trail of Tears.
I did not hold that against my wife.
I thought she'd change her mind,
but she said she was too old,
said I wasn't worth a damn and she was right.
I strayed again. Found myself another Indian gal,
a Choctaw mixed with white.
She was fourteen. I was sixty.

I thought she'd conceive, but she was barren
and died from TB when she was sixteen.
After that, I met Fannie, a full-blooded Choctaw,
who finally gave me two sons.
They both hate me.
I don't know howcome.
I only know I'm an old man now.
Looking back on ninety-five years with some remorse.
A woman is not a horse you can trade, sell or shoot
when you get tired of her.
I realize now that it's too late
a man can learn from his mistakes.
A few good women is all it takes.

DISGRACE

I was drinking scotch and water
when my daughter got home.
She was wearing the graduation dress
I bought her at JCPenney.
It looked like it had stayed on her,
and I was relieved,
because I had imagined her
lying on the backseat
of a beat up Ford
as the Martinez boy put his you know what
you know where.
The dress was too old for her,
a black, velvet sheath
with a big satin bow in front.
I told her I wouldn't buy it, but I did.
I shouldn't have.
Now I tell her, "You disobeyed me."
"I told you to be home by twelve midnight.
I don't care if you just graduated
from high school.
You are seventeen and living under my roof
and it is three o'clock in the morning.
Guess I'll have to teach you a lesson,"
I say quietly, although I want to yell.
That's when I trip over the vinyl hassock

I bought at Levitz Furniture half-off
Christmas in July sale
and fall flat on my ass.
"This is nineteen sixty-five," she says,
"not the Stone Age."
"Don't sass me," I yell finally,
as she runs in her room and slams the door.
"And don't slam that goddamn door.
It gives me a headache."
These days you can't tell a girl nothing.
She thinks she knows everything.
Got those Beatle records, them Rolling Stones
and what not.
All those white men. I don't know
what's gotten into her.
She's going down a dangerous path
on roller skates, yes she is
and I'm all that's standing between her
and disgrace.
Ever since she started men'strating,
I have dedicated my life
to keeping her from getting pregnant
out of wedlock.
All a woman's got is her good name
and there's always some worthless man
waiting to drag it through the mud.
I should know.
I didn't turn up with no bastards,
not exactly, no, but I could have
and yes, she only knows half the story
about that sonofabitch first husband of mine,

old enough to be my father,
left me alone so he could run around
with a white waitress, what was her name?
Did I ever know it?
Anyway, left me at the mercy of another man,
left me with her.
I plan to tell her the whole truth one of these days.
She's already suspicious.
Who wouldn't considering how she looks?
Took after her real father.
I just tell everybody it's our Indian blood.
"She's Indian," I say,
if anybody asks me about her,
but if you really "look" at her,
you see the Japanese.
You see Mike Ogawa, that's who,
on his knees,
taking off my penny loafers and socks,
see him kissing my toes,
so I tingle all over and go weak.
I know I shouldn't,
but I can't even open my mouth
to let his tongue in,
just have to lie back
and feel as if the whole world
is one big candy apple,
red and juicy just for me,
until reality comes knocking at the door
nine months later.
What a sound.
After Mike leaves me the last time,

I see what I've done
without the blinders on,
but it's too late.
I don't want her to end up like that.
I want her to come in the kitchen,
while I make a grilled cheese and tomato sandwich
the way I used to when she was a little girl
and it was the two of us against the world,
not just her against me,
but she won't because now I am her enemy.
I've only tried to make her see how empty
what she thinks is love can be.
That Martinez boy is half like her,
Mexican and Negro,
not a bad combo as it goes.
They'd have pretty children,
but I know he'd hurt her.
Pretty men are useless.
She needs a toothless old fool
she can control,
but some of them are cruel too
and use a young girl, yes they do.
I should let her get her kicks
on the old Route 66 of heartbreak, I guess,
but I am too old to clean up the mess,
no she's going to college.
She'll make something of herself, unlike me.
I let my chances disappear between my legs
more than once and look at me now,
doing housework,
not making enough money to dress my girl

the way she deserves.
I ought to tell her about her father,
just call her out here
but I won't, it's too soon
and tomorrow I won't speak to her either
when she gets up the courage
to ask me to pass the sugar,
as we eat our cornflakes in a silence
as loud as a slamming door
and footsteps going downstairs
on which later I take a "fall,"
to get rid of her,
but only succeed in scaring myself
into this reluctant motherhood.
After we finish, I finally croak a few words,
as if I haven't spoken for a long time.
"Dicks don't have no conscience," I tell her
and she gives me a looks that asks,
"What are you talking about?"
"I mean," I pause, thinking it should be clear.
"Mom, I'm just taking out the garbage," she says,
as I put away the past
like a wedding dress.

GREETINGS FRIEND

Choctaw, Cherokee . . .
It was all the same to me
when I was ten.
All I knew was we were Indian,
part anyway.
I couldn't tell by looking at myself.
I just saw a mouth with front teeth missing.
I always wore a red velvet shirt like a Navajo
a cowboy belt, jeans, cowboy boots
and my hair in pigtails.
When I went outside to play,
I'd whoop and holler
and pretend I was a warrior
defending my people,
until my mother called me
and my Siamese to dinner.
He ate beside the table
on the floor, of course.
Afterward, I'd go outside again
and look at my horse, Queenie.
I didn't ride because I was scared to,
but I gave her sugar,
then I stood on a stool
and scratched her head above the white star.
Sometimes she whinnied and galloped over

when she saw me.
Other times, she just ran away
as if she didn't want to be bothered
by little girls that day.
She was like my great-grandfather, John.
He lived with my great-aunt
and spent his time sitting in his room.
Once I asked him what he was doing
and he said, "Chewing on the past."
"How does it taste?" I asked.
He said, "Like sawdust,"
then he didn't say anything else.
He mostly kept to himself,
a cigar box of deeds in his lap.
I mean ashes,
because he didn't own the land anymore.
A few years before,
somebody burned down his house in Oklahoma
after he found oil.
He said he knew who'd had a hand in it,
but he was too old to fight them
and asked my great-aunt to move
him and my great-grandmother, Maggie,
to Tucson, Arizona,
which is where I was
and where he sat, a can of tobacco spit
at his feet,
the smell of it and the musty odor of old people
mixed in with something else
so suffocating I used to have to run outside
and take deep breaths

if I stayed too long.
He'd always say, "Go on and play.
I'm tired today,"
but one time, he called me back.
He said, "I got something for you,"
and he gave me a photo of an Indian man.
He said, "that's my brother.
He's named after me."
I wondered how that could be, but I didn't say so,
then he said, "Don't you see the resemblance?"
I said, "Sort of,"
and he just snorted and bit off some tobacco
and started talking about the past,
but I wasn't interested
and he said, "Go on then.
Take care of that picture,
you'll need it someday."
I was so happy to escape,
I kissed his wrinkled cheek
and didn't even need to breathe
fresh air once I got out of there.

Now I look at the photograph
and try to feel something about it,
but I can't and I can't even claim
that being fifty three has given me
some perspective on what John was doing
when he gave it to me.
"Must have been a whim of some kind," says my mother.
"You know how old people are."
Still it worries me sometimes

that I can't find the reason,
can't even find out what his brother's name really was,
unless John wasn't teasing me back then.
"I wonder if they were twins?"
"No, couldn't have been."
"John was older," mother tells me
and, "He lived like a white man."
I wonder what she means by that,
but when I ask her,
she just goes back to smoking her cigarette
and says, "Let the dead stay dead.
Anyway, I'm black and I'm proud.
I'm not an Indian anymore, if I ever was."
But I remember when she used to dress
like a Navajo too and go to powwows
and all her friends were Indians, or part.
She married black men, except for my father,
but that's another story
and I won't bother with it now.
Like Queenie, I don't have time.
I'm busy searching old census records,
land titles and such,
trying to reconstruct what was once
a living, breathing entity,
but now I realize was John's sawdust.
As I sit in his room,
which is long empty,
because when he died, they burned all his things,
I wish he'd come back, so I could ask him
what it was like to be robbed of his birthright,
if that's what it was.

But maybe he didn't think of his land that way.
Maybe he thought he was just its caretaker.
I don't know, but being so close to it all
makes me feel if I just call his name the right way,
he'll lean down from heaven,
or wherever he is and say,
"That's right, that's it. Now go on and play."
But I'm chewing on nothing but air and I know it
and my mother is saying how we're Choctaws
and we're better than these Arizona Indians
and I say, "I thought you were black,"
as she goes back to coughing just like John used to,
until she says, "Shit, who knows what I am?"
When I look in the mirror now,
I see a little girl
who can't be anyone I know,
who long ago, met Tonto at the drive-in
and said, "How" and raised her hand in greeting
and he said, "How"
and moved on to the next car,
leaving her, leaving me even then
with a slight sense of dislocation.
I remember how proud we were
that an Indian was there to meet us,
although John said we'd have been better off
staying home and going to bed early,
because a real Indian
would never say "How,"
he'd just know what to do.
I guess that means I'm not real either.
I guess I'm just pretending

and should give up and move
and let my house burn,
let my oil earn another man's living,
but I'm not giving up.
I won't be dust.
I won't just sit here,
too old to do more
than pore over charred papers
and rue the day Columbus arrived
just in time for the big giveaway.

GRANDFATHER SAYS

"Sit in my hand."
I'm ten.
I can't see him,
but I hear him breathing
in the dark.
It's after dinner playtime.
We're outside,
hidden by trees and shrubbery.
He calls it hide-and-seek,
but only my little sister seeks us
as we hide
and she can't find us,
as grandfather picks me up
and rubs his hands between my legs.
I only feel a vague stirring
at the edge of my consciousness.
I don't know what it is,
but I like it.
It gives me pleasure
that I can't identify.
It's not like eating candy,
but it's just as bad,
because I had to lie to grandmother
when she asked,
"What do you do out there?"

"Where?" I answered.
Then I said, "Oh, play hide-and-seek."
She looked hard at me,
then she said, "That was the last time.
I'm stopping that game."
So it ended and I forgot.
Ten years passed, thirty-five,
when I began to reconstruct the past.
When I asked myself
why I was attracted to men who disgusted me
I traveled back through time
to the dark and heavy breathing part of my life
I thought was gone,
but it had only sunk from view
into the quicksand of my mind.
It was pulling me down
and there I found grandfather waiting,
his hand outstretched to lift me up,
naked and wet
where he rubbed me.
"I'll do anything for you," he whispered,
"but let you go."
And I cried, "Yes," then, "No."
"I don't understand how you can do this to me.
I'm only ten years old,"
and he said, "That's old enough to know."

THE SECRET

You stand so still beside my bed,
the pillow raised above my head
while I pretend to be asleep.
I can barely keep from laughing,
but I don't want to stop playing.
I'm having so much fun.
I won't betray myself by saying,
"Mommy, see I'm still awake.
I was only fooling you,"
as you take a nickel
from your robe pocket
and lay it under my pillow,
whispering, "Willow, do you know
how much your mommy loves you?"
I know you did before the "incident."
That's what Daddy calls it.
I think it had something
to do with my baby brother, Danny,
who got taken up to Heaven
when he was three and I was eight.
I just remember his bed was empty
and you were crying beside it that time.
Afterward, Daddy took you to your bedroom.
You stayed a long time with the shades drawn
and the maid dressed me.

She combed my hair,
prepared my lunch and shook her head
when she heard your name.
Then one day I came home from school
to find you sitting on the stool
in the kitchen,
chopping carrots and celery
so you could make your famous stew.
I said, "Where's Ethel?"
"She's gone," you answered
and I said I didn't like her anyway
she smelled like wet wool and cabbage.
We had dinner like a family
but we weren't the way we used to be.
Daddy didn't notice, but I did
how you hid your tears.
When I heard you crying and went to help
you'd yell, "Are you spying on me?"
I began to stay in my room.
Other times, when I came home from school,
I'd find you prowling the hall
like a caged lion.
Back and forth you'd stalk
all the while talking about Danny
as if he were still here
and not in the grave.
I knew that's where he really was
because I'd seen him in his little casket,
then watched as they lowered it
in the ground
and heard the sound of your screams

in my bad dreams that night.
Grandmother said I should have stayed home.
I was too young to go to a funeral,
but you said, "She's got to learn that life
is just dust in the end,"
or did the reverend say that and not you?
I seem to remember adults there,
but no other children, except cousin Johnnie,
who is older than me and gets an allowance
and never sees his mother on her knees,
scrubbing the floor which isn't dirty,
because the new maid cleaned it
before she left an hour ago.
Something is wrong, but I don't know
how to tell Daddy,
So I tell my dolls and my teddy bear.
They think I should do something
and I say I will
when I am ready.
Now they are mad
and won't talk to me,
because they think I don't value their advice.
They say I'd rather ask my computer
which is only a machine.
I did log on to a Web site for teens
whose parents had died,
but it didn't help.
I tried to find one for dead brothers and sisters,
but I only got locked out by this thing
Daddy put on it for my protection.
Now I sit, facing the wall,

while Mommy calls out Danny's name,
as if he can answer.
Maybe it's a game she's playing
like the one she plays with me,
the one I pretend not to see.
Maybe Danny's only playing dead too
and there's no gash in his head,
where he was struck hard
with a glass decanter that shattered,
leaving splatters on the walls and carpet
and a trail of red down the hall
that I followed to find Mommy
lying on her back,
glass embedded in her hands.
When Daddy came home from work,
they locked me in my room
and when I came out,
everything was different
and smelled of disinfectant
and Mommy wasn't anywhere
and Danny simply wasn't there—
no clothes, no toys,
no awful smell of boy remained.
Ethel said our apartment was like a tomb
and turned on the TV, opened the curtains
and told me to make all the noise I wanted,
but after Mommy came back
I had to keep quiet.
I couldn't even chew cornflakes too loudly,
so I'd hold them in my mouth,
until the milk softened them,

then I'd swallow.
Sometimes I'd gag
and Mommy would send me to my room
where I would sit
until I learned not to disobey.
Today, she made me pray for forgiveness,
but I don't know why.
I didn't do anything wrong. Did I?
I asked and thew my glass of orange juice.
It smashed against the refrigerator.
One piece stuck in my hand
when I tried to remove it from my hair.
After I started to cry, Mommy did too,
then she said, "It's not you, not you."
Everything was fine,
until Daddy had to drag her away from my bed.
"Your mother's tired," was all he said.
The next day, she was gone again.
Ethel was back
and I decided maybe I should pray,
so I knelt in front of my dolls and Teddy
and confessed my sin,
because I was ready.
They told me they always knew the truth.
I can't hide anything from them.
I tried and failed and Mommy knows too,
but she'll never tell.
Cross my heart and hope to die
I never will either.

INTERCOURSE

for John Kennedy, Jr.

The water is a cold fire I swallow,
thinking it tastes like blood,
as I rise to the surface.
I'm saved, I think, as my head
emerges from the waves,
then everything disappears in a gray haze
that smells of smoke and sizzling flesh.
I choke, spit out bits of bone.
I'm surprised to see a mermaid
sitting on a smooth black stone.
I tell her I'm lost
and she throws me a rope of long, blonde hair,
but when I grab hold,
she pokes me with a trident
and I fall back into pure hopelessness.
I drift that way a long time,
until I find myself in your bedroom.
I inhale the perfume of your sleep,
a combination of baby powder and almond oil,
trying to keep from waking you as I breathe deeply,
but you open your eyes
and I am seized by the need to confess
all the things I've ever kept secret,
but I can't remember what they are,

so I settle for idle conversation.
I mastered the art of seeming ordinary, I tell you,
but you don't respond.
Is that why you don't recognize me, I continue,
content to hear the sound of my own voice,
though it's filled with weariness
and a chilly intimacy,
which seems to increase
with each breath I take.
"I rose from the dead just for you," I say finally
and that seems to move you,
as a tear slides down your cheek
and seeks refuge under the sheet,
pulled up to your chin,
as if it can keep me from getting too close.
Didn't you cry for me over green tea and poppy-seed cake?
Didn't you make a pilgrimage to the botanical gardens
and sit meditating over my fate,
as if you could make sense of your own life
by summoning mine, or am I mistaken?
I loved how you stared at my photographs, I say,
and endless film footage of me
leading my life in the public eye,
as if I had no idea I was being watched.
My inamorata, I'll do anything, I whisper,
as I take your hand
and press it against my erection.
At last, you seem to wake
from your enchanted sleep,
then wrest your hand from mine,
asking, "How can you dress like this?"

Is that any way to talk to your prince?
I admit I'm not wearing Armani,
but what difference does it make now?
You ask if I have proof I'm who I say I am.
You can't believe I'd appear to you
wearing white chinos, white opennecked shirt
with the sleeves rolled up,
my feet bare, my toenails painted dark red.
I turn my head in profile.
See. Death only enhanced my beauty.
I'm still John.
I'm still living on in your dreams,
as horny and ordinary as any guy on a first date,
who can't say, or do anything right,
but feels he must prove he can.
You're not amused.
You think you can do better
and I sink into a puddle of saltwater,
as you finally relent and call my name.
It's too late. I came and went
in the same instant it took you to realize
you'd captured your prize only to lose him
as he slipped between your thighs,
but could not penetrate the sealed landscape,
where celebrity creates an alternate reality.
There fact and fiction lie
one atop the other fucking furiously,
when one surrenders unconditionally,
the other dies.

TRUE LOVE

I absorb you through my skin,
then exhale you like a breath held too long.
I inhale again, air scented like cloves, oranges and musk,
by the candles I bought just for tonight,
as you slide your fingers inside me,
pull them out and wipe them on my thigh.
My fluid dries in the breeze
from the fan that does not cool.
Ninety-five degrees and nothing
to ease us back from the precipice,
where we stand, staring down.
We end here tonight,
or descend from the heights of passion
to become a couple.
You look into my eyes,
trying to read my desire,
as if it will tell you what to do.
You put your hand in the fire
and now it's burning you,
turning you into another one of my possessions.
It's what you want. If you didn't
you wouldn't beg to be poured into my mouth.
I press your face down
and say, "That's where I am."
You get up after I'm done, wash and dress

and I lie watching you,
waiting for you to give me a sign you'll come back.
"You're destroying me," you say.
I can't stay away from you and it's too much.
I can't work, or think about anything
but how sweet you taste
and that place where you put your hand last time.
"You mean up your ass?" I say,
delighting in being crass,
provoking you, a pastime of mine.
"I won't let you make me the villain of this B movie.
Why don't you go home to Mommy,
but you can't fuck her, can you?"
That gets to you. I knew it would.
You slam the door on the way out
of our favorite hotel room
in Bisbee, Arizona.
Our vacation in hell, if you ask me,
but you love the atmosphere,
love the "primitiveness" of it.
No air-conditioning, dial phones,
an old-fashioned iron bed
and a small black-and-white TV, no cable.
Just you, just me.
"Nothing between us and our lust," you said,
but there is, isn't there?
It's eternity. It's the thing always out there
when people start caring about each other.
It smothers love eventually,
yet we need it.
We pursue it single-mindedly.

I lie in bed contentedly, despite my unease,
thinking maybe you freed yourself from me this time,
until I hear your key in the lock,
then I turn, facing the mirrored bathroom door
and pretend to be asleep,
imagining how tomorrow you'll be so glad
I didn't see you raise the heavy, glass ashtray
above my head for a few minutes,
before you put it back on the table
and admitted to yourself at last
that you belong to me.

RUDE AWAKENING

The first time I saw Clotilde,
she was standing in the window
of an Amsterdam brothel,
her negligee discretely buttoned
from head to toe,
so I had to use my imagination.
I liked that, liked how she beckoned me
with one long, scarlet fingernail.
"Follow me," it said and I obeyed.
Before I met her,
I taught high school English in Rapid City
and coached volleyball
and most of the time
I didn't even think about my nights
lying alone in bed, smoking,
watching the red lights of my alarm clock.
Last July, I got an insurance check,
because I wrecked my car
and I decided to use the money
to do some things I'd always dreamed about.
My buddy, Art, the Assistant Principal
and I went to London, Rome, Paris
and I allowed him to harrass me
into going to see the prostitutes of Amsterdam.
He said, "Frank, are you a man?"

I answered, "Yes, I am,"
and so we went to take a look and look we did.
He was sensible.
He partook, but did not take out
more than he put in,
but then he didn't fall in love
and have to spend so many nights
waiting for his beloved to get off work
and do for free what she was paid to do
simply because she loved me
and not because she wanted my money.
I swear there was nothing to make me suspicious
and it was so exciting with her
that I did not acknowledge what I knew
deep in my heart
and so in my mind escaped total complicity
in the thing that came to be my ruination.
Clotilde's gone now,
she's just the breeze
that chills me this autumn afternoon
when instead of teaching,
I'm lying in bed, trying to understand
why I chose to accept the disgrace of losing my job
and not to fight, not to present myself
to the school board as a victim of her deceit
as an answer to the complaints
about the company I was keeping.
Art, being the SOB I'd once mistaken for a friend,
decided to tell the secret
I had not failed to share with him,
so overcome was I by passion.

I never thought we'd end our friendship
over that thin, slip of a girl
just because she had a penis.
I ask you, what is wrong with the company of men?
If I had read the guidebook that said,
"If you visit one of the women,
we would like to remind you
that they are not always women,"
I wonder now if I would have faced it all sooner
and left my darling back in the window,
posing as if for a Rembrandt tableau
in which a slightly overweight, middle aged man
pretends to practice the art of letting go
and does not notice
what is so obvious to those
whose vision is not obstructed
by the rose-colored glasses
behind which with eyes closed tightly
he kisses the throat of his loved one
and runs his tongue over the apple there
and knows everything at once.
Don't we all want a little mystery
with our romance,
even if it is accompanied
by a rude awakening,
when you find in your hand
the kind of surprise
that might disgust any other man,
but only made me wonder at fate
and how it sends us the mate we always wanted,
if only we could admit it.

GENDER/BENDER

for Chip

Men used to call me "Beauty."
They all wanted me
and I let them run their hands
over my body
and taste the anisette of it,
but they meant nothing to me,
while you mean everything.
I asked my friends for help.
I even asked my mother.
I said, "Is he my soul mate,
he can't be, can he,
isn't it a mistake
and how can I make it go away?"
He can't give me what I want.
He loves me in his way
which is to say
within the limits of his sexual orientation.
The one experience he had with a woman
when he was seventeen
was a disaster, he tells me,
as he takes my hand out of the blue.
We are getting ready to go to a party
and like any other couple,
we stand in front of the mirror,

checking our reflections for imperfections.
True, I have stood with other men,
both clothed and naked,
but never in love like this,
in love enough to make me wish
I were a man,
so I could stand naked with him,
running my hands over him, erect and quivering,
before licking him from neck to feet,
then back up to meet his lips in a kiss
that nullifies all other kisses
and defies the limits of our bodies.
I could wear a strap-on dildo (why not?).
They make them so lifelike now.
Would he know the difference
if he were blindfolded
and didn't touch me?
Would he somehow feel the subtle presence
of a woman assuming the disguise
of a man's desire?
Once a fire's lit,
it burns until it's out.
Could he stop me
once I put my tongue inside his mouth
even when he tastes my lipstick?
Or maybe he'd think I was a cross-dresser,
a transsexual,
or some other hypertextual combination.
Would I be me, or just a version
he could tolerate
for a furtive and exciting assignation,

a vacation from himself perhaps
when he relaxes into a new identity,
not knowing who is he and who is she,
only knowing me,
as I sit astride him,
as he lies face down, moaning into his pillow,
"What a man. You are so powerful.
And sensitive."
I know I should give up
and accept the fact that he is homosexual,
so clinical, but accurate,
so unromantic
and lacking the thrust of poetry.
Love is just love,
until it's physical,
then often it turns cynical and violent.
I'm better off without that loss of dignity.
But maybe I "should" drink that poison once again
and on the brink of dying
send my spirit flying into him,
but ooh la la I mustn't forget we're friends,
not lovers, not enemies,
just in between extremes,
safe in our dangerous dreams.

FIFTY-THREE

"I never thought I'd end up a hard blonde," I said,
"Did you?"
My friend, Sue, looked at me, just looked,
then went to pee
and I settled down to think about it,
but first, I ordered another round.
"Bartender, I mean Brad," I yelled,
over the hell-raising boys
bellied up at the bar, "Fill 'er up."
This round's on Sue, who's back
from the restroom now,
hair combed and sprayed
and there's a chalky place under her left eye,
where she put too much concealer,
but I'm too depressed to tell her about it
and I just lick salt from my lips
and knock back another shot of tequilla.
"That shit'll kill you," says Sue,
as she downs another scotch on rocks.
Scotch on cocks, I call it,
but she doesn't get it and I let it slide.
She's my best friend now and then
when I'm beside myself
and about to do something terrible.
She can always tell

and says, let's get the hell out of town,
which means let's go down to the Shamrock Bar,
where the drinks keep coming
like I used to,
before the change got through with me.
Now I have to fantasize
like nobody's business
just to get set and go.
Ask my last boyfriend, that no good sonofabitch,
who ditched me for a younger, dumber version
of guess who?
Boy is he in for a surprise
once her eggs dry up
and she starts to look a little tired about the eyes,
her hair starts thinning
and when men look past her
as if she isn't there.
I'm here, though, like an itch
that won't go away
and here I'll stay
on a stool at the end of the bar,
where I can see everybody who comes in,
hoping one of them will take me
down memory lane and leave me there.
Twenty-three and raring to see what's next,
as I sit on some guy's face,
but every hair in place,
as I yell my own name,
because I love myself too much
to ever love anyone else.
But that'll never happen now.

Now I sit watching the shitty night unfolding
as fast as it can,
knowing I won't be holding anything in my hand tonight
but another drink and a bottle of Percodan,
daring myself to do it one more time.

PASSAGE

for Allen Ginsberg

Sunflowers beside the railroad tracks,
sunflowers giving back the beauty God gave you
to one lonely traveler
who spies you from a train window
as she passes on her way to another train station.
She wonders if she were like you
rooted to your bit of earth
would she be happy,
would she be satisfied
to have the world glide past and not regret it?
For a moment, she thinks so,
then decides that, no, she never could
and turns back to her book of poetry,
remembering how hard it was to get here
and that flowers have their places as people do
and she cannot simply exchange hers for another,
even though she wants it.
That's how it is.
Her mother told her.
Now she believes her,
although she wishes she didn't.
At fifty-three, she feels the need
to rebel against the inevitable winding down.
She already feels it in her bones,

feels artery deterioration, and imagines
cancerous indications on medical charts
she hopes will never be part of her life,
as she turns back to the window
to catch the last glimpse of the sunflowers
that sent her thoughts on a journey
from which she knows she will never return,
only go on and on
and then just go.

LULLABY

Run my child. Don't delay.
The beast is beating on the door
with rifle butt and fists.
Soon his boots are stomping
on the floor, as if he's cold
and trying to warm his feet.
He hasn't had a thing to eat for days
and tears bread from your sister's hand
before he shoots her in the head
and smashes all the dishes.
His mouth full, he chews
as he ascends the stairs
two at a time and finds me
calmly sitting on the bed.
"Waiting for me?" he asks,
as he hurls a stone
that strikes me in the face,
breaking my jaw,
then proceeds to set fire to my body,
after which he walks back downstairs and outside.
The hound howls as the neighbors
steal what's left of us.
We're dead afterall.
Who cares whether or not we suffered
or even that they once called us friends,

because in the end they agree
we got what we deserved for being born.
I hoped you would survive,
but you die anyway beside the road
your body frozen to the earth
until spring,
when your bones are discovered by the hound
who buries them with other bones
he's collected as he roams the countryside
masterless now and wild.
He's forgotten he once was companion to a child,
who used to scratch him between the ears.
Now that spot is inflamed
and he shakes his head and rubs it against a tree
beside the stream where we picnicked
and he stood on his hind legs,
almost dancing as he begged for scraps
of boiled ham, dark bread and deviled eggs.
Now when he hears the sound of voices,
he growls, covers the bones quickly
and hides beneath the burned-out shell of a car
until they fade
like all the voices that once made us family,
but could not save us from our destiny.

THE BROKER

Twins are good luck.
In my country, a boy and a girl especially.
Two boys equals double support,
but two girls I am sorry to report
are looked on as burdens.
Of course, sometimes the stars
are inclined to bestow
more bounteous fortune on a family
than they might ordinarily
and twins of any and/or either sex
are blessed by being born
under a sign
that is cause for rejoicing
rather than for mourning.
Your twins, fortunately, are a boy and girl.
You cannot in all the world
find any two more compatible with you,
They are not from my country, no.
I acquired them, shall we say, in Mexico.
They speak no English,
although they know the words,
"please," and "thank you,"
which I taught them,
because I felt it might
make them a bit more acceptable

to a respectable person like you.
Americans appreciate courtesy.
I know that now that I am an American
and no longer let astrology,
or superstition rule my life,
no, I let my daily planner do that
and it is telling me
that I have another appointment
in exactly thirty minutes,
so if you're ready
we can retrieve the children.
They will be so grateful to receive you
and will repay you a thousand times
for choosing me to be your procurer.
That word does not offend me,
because it describes perfectly
the service I provide
for discerning customers
who want a bit of the exotic in their lives.
The downpayment you wired to my bank
is earning interest
and I appreciate your advice on investments.
One has to think of the future,
even if one finds it unpleasant.
I used to live from day to day,
but I realize that isn't the way it is here,
where fear of starvation
or some other tribulation is less common
than among my countrymen.
Where are my keys?
Ah, here they are glittering like stars

above the ocean
the night my brother offered to stake me with—
Oh, yes, I know you're anxious to get going.
You're a busy person.
So am I
and what is worse than hearing boring stories
about someone else's struggles.
I know, I know it is difficult
to juggle your duties.
I have the same problem myself.
Anyway, come children,
come say goodbye to uncle.
What? Oh, it's just a term
one uses in my country.
One learns to do what one has to
in order to make things run smoothly
don't you think?
Remember if you find that you desire
another foray into uncharted waters
I am at your service.
All sales are final.
Thank you.

THE CALLING

I promised I'd be good that day
and go to missionary school,
but the bad man still came to punish me.
My mother begged him to spare my life,
but he said, "Woman, I am Africa
and Africa takes what it wants."
He opened a box and she looked inside,
then she screamed and fell to her knees.
Before I knew what was happening,
pain shot a fiery bullet into my arm.
When I came to, I was surprised
for my whole body told me I died
when death shook my hand.
My mother burned the stump to cauterize it.
Is healing agony? It must be, I decided,
as I lay in the strange quiet of morning.
Not even a cock crowed,
no women went to get water for cooking,
no scent of plaintains and stew
blew into our hut.
I shut my eyes and tried to ride
the waves of nausea,
flowing through my body
to someplace where suffering did not exist,
but it was useless.

Again and again, I returned to the place
where my hand, clenched in a fist
lay in a box with other hands
in various states of decay.
When my mother shook me awake,
I knew what I would do.
"Get me a knife," I told her.
I began to practice slicing melons
with one hand,
until I could take my place
beside the man who's like a father to me now,
as we wander around, demanding reparations
in pounds of flesh.
In the villages, they call me "The Chopper,"
and they say it with respect.

THE WHITE HOMEGIRL

My mom liked back roads, side roads,
high roads and low.
She didn't know much, but she knew go.
Once she got started, she wouldn't slow down
until she was out and she was out a lot.
I understood, though. She got depressed
'cause people fucked with her, people did
and she'd take a break, relieve some stress
then she'd be fine for a while,
get clean, get a job.
They couldn't tame a girl like her, like me,
but they tried. She'd tell me
to be strong like the brothers
who could give her what she needed,
the ones who only sold
and didn't partake of the product.
When she scored, I'd wait around for her outside.
Sometimes I'd find another kid
in the same typea situation.
Tyronne was last time.
He helped me with my homework
while mom was whoring inside.
Anyway, that was a long time ago, like twelve years.
I was ten then. I wasn't scared
when the big shit finally happened and Mom OD'd.

I got put in a foster home.
Boy was I ever glad to move outta there
when I came "of age."
I'd always been of age. They just didn't know it
and now I don't do no dope, I don't 'ho.
I work at Jack n' Box, Taco Bell, you know
until I get restless, then I rolls
with my homies.
You can always find a few discarded like condoms
by their parents who maybe got caught up in somethin'
they didn't know how to get out of and you,
you just along for the ride.
Like Tyronne, Baby Ruth and Chantel, my homies
we just going, well, that's my moms, that's my pops.
We don't make excuses, I mean I didn't.
Now I'm the kind of woman she would have been,
made for friendship, not sex,
with my flat ass, my flat chest
and a big mouth
that gets me in trouble
I can always get out of,
'cause I'm smart
and know how to start something and finish it.
See me "rope a dope" around the coke, the "herine,"
the mainline to nowhere.
Honey, I been there
and I'm not going back,
not even to get my mother's body.

THE GREENWOOD CYCLE

after the events surrounding the Tulsa Riots

1. CONJURE

I thought I was dreaming,
when I saw the sky fulla black smoke,
but I wasn't, no, 'cause I pinched myself
and it hurt
and I knew we were gonna suffer
for somebody's sinfulness.
"Just like Jesus," you said, Mama,
when you screamed,
"Run, daughter, run,
white men are comin', they got guns."
I said, "I see 'em, Mama, I see,
they ridin' up and down the street
throwin' torches on rooftops, on porches,
on the poor Negro trying to pray
while the flames eat him up
they so hungry.
Mama, we can't get away."
"Run on, daughter," you cried, "hide if you can
from the white devil,"
but he wasn't no devil, he was a man
and he was evil, yes, he was,
but he wasn't supernatural,

he didn't have no power to conjure like I do,
when I conjure you,
crying, "Don't look back, or you'll turn to ashes
and fall down among the dead in Greenwood."

Now I'm alone
and I don't say nothing 'bout it to nobody,
just fix me a hot toddy
and sit rocking in my rocker
and think about you, Mama,
turned to dust
wrapped in a dirty sheet
with a body lying on top.
"It ain't Christian, is it," you whisper,
"to be murdered like this and just forgot?"
I rock in time
to the ticktock of the grandfather clock
you dragged from the burning house,
because it was your daddy's,
give to him by the old master
when your daddy got freedom.
For some reason, it didn't burn up
just charred a bit,
a piece of wood pried off it.
When I got up the money,
I went and bought it off the junkman,
who thought it was worth something.
It was, but only to me,
rusted, permanently stopped
at the hour and the minute
that cost me you.

2. SANCTUARY

"Is the world on fire?"
—Sister of Mr. Beard, survivor

I said, "Brother, the world's on fire."
He said, "Liar,"
but Daddy said, "Y'all climb on up higher
in that tree so only God can see you,
not me, or the white man running thisa way,
guns blazing, burning up everything.
Can't see nothing through the smoke,
can't breathe, choking like I got two hands
around my throat.
Je-e-e-sus, Je-e-e-sus."
"Brother," I whispered, and he said, "Hush,"
as a hot wind rustled the leaves
and the white man ran past,
screaming something about niggers and too much—
"What'd he say, brother?" I asked,
but he turned away.
"Lookayonder," I heard him say,
just as a loud crack and a popping sound
got mixed up in my head.
When I climbed down that old tree, I said,
"Brother, are you dead?"
He just stared at me,
then outta nowhere someone grabbed my hair.
Daddy had braided it for me that morning
and tied a ribbon on it
and said, "I'm warning you don't take it off,"

and I didn't, but it come off anyway,
when the hand jerked too hard
and got a fist fulla red ribbon
and I started running myself.
Wasn't nobody else but me around after 'while
in the dark, back in the back of somebody's house,
I mean underneath it,
where a dog was hiding too.
It was a hound dog with two pups.
You know how mean a new mother can be,
but she didn't growl, or nothing,
just gave me the eye
and went on back to nursing
and didn't do nothing when I got real close
and stroked her fur and closed my eyes.
I woke to her sighs.
The pups' eyes weren't open yet,
but they moved their heads
when I started to crawl outta hiding,
but then I heard crying, I heard a shot
and moved on back
and got close to the dog and those pups.
I knew from that moment on
I was hound Mary's daughter
and I would never leave.

3. THE RESCUE

I seen trouble coming from a long way off.
I seen it this morning in a bubble of blood
when I cut my finger on that cup I broke.
Nobody had to tell me about it.
I could see things. I had second sight.
Got it from Mama, a full-blooded Cherokee.
"Son," she'd say, "you got one foot in Heaven
the other in Hell
trouble gonna find you
wherever you dwell.'
It's gonna come in fire.
I know secrets I better not tell
and you will too, when the time comes."
Here it is—
a Negro boy running fast as he can
a white man behind him
with a noose in his hand.
My daddy was Negro too.
Should I do something 'cause halfa me
could also swing from a tree?
I don't know what to do
til I remember Mama telling me
about the long walk
when so many died on the Trail of Tears.
She said the old folks told her
nobody could believe Andrew Jackson
would make them leave their home, but he did.
The white man takes what he gives.
He's got two faces and both of them smile

while he plans your destruction.
"He don't like Indians, but he hates Negroes," she said.
"You got looks and hair like your mother
you're lucky that way,
defer to the white man, stay out of his path."
"But I can't Mama," I say out loud,
"Can't let a child die like this.
It ain't right, is it?"
She answered, all right,
well, it was the wind,
but it was her voice talking through it.
I got in the wagon, all hitched 'cause I was going somewhere
and turned my mules in the path
where the white man was running and stopped there.
Gave that boy enough time to hide someplace.
White man cursed, pointed his gun at me.
"Sorry Mister," I said,
"these mules got minds of their own."
"Ain't you part nigger?" He said to me,
then he shot my mules.
I knew he'd die in his sleep.
I saw the sowing he'd reap
and that released me from my hatred.
I buried Brandy and Brandywine
took a long time, said a few words.
One day, that boy came to see me.
He had a scar running down one side of his face.
He said, "Mister, I'm cold and hungry,
can I stay at your place?"
I said, "Yes, come on in the kitchen where it's warm.
Lemme look at your face.

Maybe I got something that'll help,"
but he said, "Nothing will."
I filled his plate with pinto beans, bacon, cornbread,
filled his glass of milk to the brim,
then we said grace.
"Where's your mama?" I asked
and he said, "Dead,
Yours?"
"Same. Pitiful, isn't it?
You aim to move on, or stay?"
"Don't you know?" he asked.
I said, "Some things, not others."
He said, "Your mother was a witch,
that's what people say."
"Naw, she wasn't, she just saw things."
"I ain't too black for you?"
"I am too," I said.
"No, you ain't," he answered,
"but you'll do."

4. THE SHERIFF'S EXPLANATION

I deputized a lot of men that day.
I didn't say, "Are you men in the Klan,"
when they raised their hands
and swore to uphold the law.
All I cared about
was whether they were willing to die.
If they did so in the service of the white race,
I could live with that.
I could not live with the disgrace
of allowing Negroes to get away
with rape, murder and worse.
If we didn't stop them now, I thought,
we'd have to later.
Yes, innocent died,
depending on how you look at it.
You couldn't tell who was what.
Miss Mary, old woman
used to cook dinner for us
when I was a boy
got caught in the middle of gunfire.
I drug her body out of the way of trampling feet,
least I could do,
but see, she was one of them.
That's what it came down to in the end.
I threw her body in the hole with the rest.
I stood there awhile,
watching the others bury that sad affair.
Mary was a kind old girl.

She liked to tickle me and make me laugh,
but I couldn't say that, could I?
She was as black as the iron skillet
she fried chicken in, her face gleaming
like it had been polished with a jeweler's cloth.
She called me her baby
and she rocked me to sleep,
but I didn't say a word when that old boy
hit her body with a rock
and said, "Another one dead,"
and told me if I needed any more help
he was ready.
I didn't have anything to say. It was over.
From then on, we avoided talking about it
the way people do when they're ashamed,
but we weren't ashamed, no, not that.
We were justified.

THE PSYCHIC DETECTIVE: IDENTITY

I follow the blood trail from the front door,
down the dark hall with the pristine walls,
only to find upon entering the kitchen,
the kind of crime scene I can sink my teeth into
if that's the right term to use
and it isn't and I know it,
but back to the action, or my reaction
which is not to show it,
but to go about my business,
because I am a professional
and this is not a confessional,
but I repeat, a crime scene
complete with corpse
slumped beside the sliding glass door
in the patio, set up for a party,
judging from the paper plates, styrofoam cups
on the picnic table under colored lights.
Who did they burn for tonight, I wonder,
then I don't because I won't let myself.
I have to focus on the dear departed
now entering a state of rigor mortis.
I sniff the air. There it is,
the smell of death,

or is it my own sweat, my own fear
beaten down to its knees,
so I can do what needs to get done,
so I can walk through blood,
as if it's nothing but a slight inconvenience,
so I can show this corpse how bad I am,
a man with a badge and a gun isn't afraid
of anyone and by God I'm not, I tell myself,
as I shut off the water in the sink.
Did the killer get thirsty
from all that dirty work?
Did he take a drink, then sink his teeth
into her, because that looks like a bite
on her right thigh and there on her breast.
Did he break the rules this time
and mix business with pleasure,
which is why he got so mad he broke the pattern
of his attacks and mutilated her,
or was it another monster who attacked,
having read enough about the other
to want to imitate, then outdo him
and embark on his own
secession from the human race?
But who am I kidding? It could have been anything
the devil, a dog or a devil dog
ordering him to do his bidding
and not the cold, calculating killer
who left her with her pubis artistically exposed,
because he's an artist, I suppose,
at least he thinks he is
and like any artist, he has an ego

as big as Texas, and a tattoo of a rose
on his shoulder. That's the only description
we've got of our homicidal lothario
and that's why they call him "The Florist."
He makes his fatal delivery
of one American Beauty Rose for each killing.
There are five beside the body
in their little containers of water.
I know it's water, because it's been tested
and will be again, but it's plain old H_2O
I'd bet on it
and nobody bets against a sure thing, right?
Anybody in Vegas can tell you they do all the time
and I'm just blowing smoke.
I'm waiting for my partner
to poke his head in the door
and tell me there's another body this time,
which I already know, because I'm psychic
and sensed the absence of completion, of letting go.
In the garage, on the front seat
of the old Dodge Dart,
a body, rather, parts of it
are laid out like cuts of meat.
"Where're the flowers?" he asks,
but I just stare, then point.
There it is, there
and it is. Body parts are laid out
in the shape of the rose my partner couldn't find.
He's getting symbolic on us, I say,
wiping a spiderweb from my face.
He'll be harder to trace now,

because he knows one mistake
and he'll fall through the ice
of his own existence.
He has no regrets now.
He's conquered his conscience
and come to a place where all is killing
and killing is all.
I know my partner thinks I'm bullshitting.
"Stinks in here," he says,
then steps out for some fresh air,
but I'm ok where I am.
I can think here. Like him
I can see the girl coming up the walk,
talking to her mother.
She's sixteen. She's carrying a birthday cake.
There's a gap between her teeth.
He's heard it's a sign of appetite
and he wonders if that's true.
Maybe she'll prove it,
if he does it right.
I get dizzy all at once
and lean against the fender.
I don't want to see anymore.
I just want to shut the door on the evil
that greets me each day with its pants down,
saying, "Look at it, look at me
and see yourself."

THE PSYCHIC DETECTIVE: FANTASY

The victim is lying on her side
as if trying to hide the imprint
of the boot heel that smashed her cheek.
As the river runs through her wounds
(and there are many)
I am coldly examining her body this morning.
"What do you think, Bob?" I ask my partner.
"Do you think she was out shopping?
See that empty shopping bag there
the one from that fancy mall."
"Who cares?" he says.
"She's dead, end of story."
It isn't ordinary as crimes go,
because she's so mutilated.
He hated her naturally,
because he imagined that she was his mother,
or some other female who wronged him
and he's in payback mode,
cracked her skull maybe with a bat,
probably his kid's. "What do you say, Bob?"
He shrugs. Psychology is not his thing.
He likes putting it together
like a math problem he can solve by adding one plus two,

but that doesn't work with psychos.
They hide from the average crime solver.
Somebody like me has to go down into hell with them
and bring them back,
even though they're radioactive with an evil
that clings to your skin.
I'm still hot from the last crime.
Hear the crackle and pop
as I pass through the mind of this killer.
There he is on his knees, his eyes filled with a red glow.
He has to pee and does into the water
that runs over her shattered face,
then he zips up, he leaves
just as the sun rises as big and as orange
as those lollipops
his mom used to buy him
when the first urge to destroy
made him tear apart his toy rabbit.
No, it was her, naked, her big breasts
swinging over him that first set him off,
as she bent down to say good night
as he lay in bed,
the odor of alcohol and a fight with his dad
suffocating him, making him reach up
and pinch the nipple inches from his face.
His mom said, "Suck on it, go ahead,
if you're man enough."
He wasn't then, but he is now
and I'm on his trail.
I'm going to swallow him
like the whale did Jonah.

Who am I kidding? He's gone, Bob.
I won't catch this one,
because he's disappeared into the ether
of ordinary life.
Can't you feel it?
This kill wasn't planned.
It was some kind of posttraumatic thing
where a scent, a sound, maybe a glance
threw him into his murderer's trance
and he entered his mother's spread thighs,
his eyes closed tightly
as he felt those breasts press against his head
like two feather pillows, so soft, so . . .
Then he came out of it
in his driveway.
His rosebushes, his azaleas,
the big cedar tree
and the kid's swing reassured him
that what had happened
was only a fantasy
and he told himself so over and over,
even as he cleaned a few remaining drops of blood
from his hands,
then watered his rosebushes
and greeted his wife with a kiss
when she came home from the store.
He did not acknowledge, or go near that door
behind which his mother
said, "Just once more, son, once more"
and he tried, he really did,
before he fell asleep,

only to wake in his own bed
and tell himself he'd had a bad dream
and leave it at that
and leave us with another unsolved murder,
another body to send to the morgue
to be claimed by relatives
who'll never have another peaceful day like his
when it's hard to believe he's the one who's alive
and not on the other side
with that girl he met at the mall and his mother
beating on a door
even the psychic detective can't open.

THE PSYCHIC DETECTIVE: DIVINITY

He stepped out of the dark.
He *was* the dark
with his chloroform, his duct tape.
He'd been waiting since dawn,
but he really hadn't been, maybe an hour
after a long hot shower,
steam seeping into every pore of his body.
The body wash after,
damask rose and sandalwood.
He liked to smell good.
It countered the other odor just enough
to soothe and calm the prey
until they recognized him for who he was.
I knew the smell mixed in
with the thin metallic odor
on the victim's clothes
folded so carefully
and laid beneath her head
and in her hands a rosary
of large black beads,
the kind the nuns at St. Anthony's
wore on their wide black leather belts,
when I was twelve

and doing time in Catholic school
which answers questions possibly
about the villain of this piece.
Perhaps the victim's death
helped ease some guilt
he'd carried with him,
while talking with friends,
wearing a slight smile,
a twinkle in his eyes
for this was a guy of guys,
not the type you'd imagine
who would kill
until something unleashed the will to murder.
Was it seeing the nuns
gliding down the esplanade at dusk,
the musk of sanctity
too much for him to bear
as the memory of some incident
returned to him with such a vengeance
he had no choice but to act and save himself!
She was the sacrifice he made
to his depraved self
and he is, believe me.
Father Thomas told him so
in confession when he was thirteen
and after a night of touching himself
he let go at last
when he imagined how it would feel
to choke his little sister.
He confessed
and was given absolution.

Father Thomas said,
"One hundred Hail Mary's, Kevin
and ask your mother to come see me."
His mother never went to Mass.
His father did
and the priest hadn't said to ask him,
so he said nothing about it,
only avoided the confessional
and when his parents separated,
he never went to Mass again.
Kevin often caught his father
looking at him in such a way
it made him wonder
but then one day his father was gone,
taking his little sister.
He stayed with his mother
and made the best of it
and never wondered much about
that fit of adolescent sexual confusion
or whatever it was
that had made him confess in the first place.
Better to keep quiet about such impulses,
about the riot of feelings
which assualted him
for years until the night
they overwhelmed him
and overcame the obstacle
to the desire he'd tried to ignore.
It was a fire, it was burning him
like the need to preach and convert.
Bob laughs and shakes his head

and asks me if I've been drinking
and says, "He's just a warped little shit
who gets his kicks by killing.
Don't you get tired of being a willing conduit
for their sickness?"
"I do, but I swore I'd use my gift to help others
and if this is the price, then so be it.
I have no choice anyway.
When I tried to stop, remember,
you called me back?
You needed my expertise to catch
that guy who liked to slice, dice
and can his victims.
Remember how we found the pantry,
the smell?
Who could stand still for that?"
Bob doesn't answer,
just waves to the forensics people
to come do their stuff
now that I've profiled the perp
and am ready for further study
in my own way,
which is to say
by tracing him backward from today,
then forward into the gray afternoon
descending on us now,
when he climbs the steps of the cathedral
stands inside the nave
for the time it takes to say
one hundred Hail Mary's,
then simply walks away.

THE PSYCHIC DETECTIVE: DESTINY

A nightlight in the shape of a bear
burns in the center of my darkness.
It's clear acrylic and inside, a blue bulb
casts a pale blue light in the room,
where I lie awake,
my twelve-year-old insomnia,
a warning of future sleepless nights.
In the rest of the house,
the lights are out.
My mother is asleep
in her room across the hall
and in the twin bed next to mine,
my little sister also sleeps,
although occasionally she says a few words
I can't quite catch.
They're like snatches of a song
you can't forget,
you can't remember either, yet . . .
They haunt me now,
as I kneel in the cathedral,
where I was baptised
and where the memorial for my sister
was conducted.

I say memorial because she was—
her body was never found.
But to achieve a sense of closure
(those were my mother's words)
the family, friends and concerned citizens
were herded into church
to listen to the priest say a few words.
He looked like a bird of prey.
I mean the way he hovered over the pulpit,
his crooked beak of a nose
and furrowed brow so vulture-like,
as he used his words as if somehow
they could conjure a body out of sound
and place it in front of us.
He said she was there in spirit,
so I thought she hadn't gone to purgatory afterall.
She wasn't bad enough to go to Hell,
well, I didn't think so.
I didn't know. I did know someone
had entered our room.
I'd heard stealthy footsteps,
the pause outside our door before he entered
and shut my eyes, barely breathing,
hoping the flutter of my eyelids
wouldn't give me away.
I wasn't afraid.
I'd been waiting all night.
I knew I'd be all right,
oh, I'd seen that too.
Don't ask how I knew. I just did.
I like the term second sight,

because it emphasizes that you "see,"
but with another kind of vision.
I heard my sister sigh,
then heard a deeper muffled sigh,
felt a hot breath against my cheek,
a chuckle and a voice whispering, "Don't peek."
I didn't dare.
"I don't need to," I almost cried,
but realized I'd be lost too,
if I didn't play dead,
so I lay still until dawn,
when I turned over and looked at the empty bed,
then fell into a deep sleep
and dreamed I understood the words
my sister had mumbled the night before
to wake finally to my mother's screams.
"It was the boogeyman," I told her,
but she didn't listen
and I chose to keep silent,
although I knew he'd taken my sister
and buried her alive in his backyard.
I'd even gasped for breath that morning
over breakfast alone at the table,
while the police asked my mother
whether I were able to tell her anything.
I tried, but I couldn't breathe,
so she put me in her bed
and I lay there until darkness covered me
like a baby blanket.
Now as I kneel without praying,
I am looking for a different boogeyman,

but he won't come inside.
He'll just stand with his hand
suspended above the holy water,
which he will not touch,
a slight smile playing about his lips,
because he thinks he's clever.
He thinks it's all clear now,
that he can go back to how it was,
before he decided to go for broke
and let out the monster
who had urged him to choke his sister years ago.
He thinks he's safe from discovery,
because he stands beyond
the outstretched arms of the statue of Christ
upon the altar where I kneel,
but he's wrong.
I gave up hiding long ago
to seek absolution for not saving my sister
and with each case I take,
I hope I'll reach some closure of my own.
I'd known the boogeyman would come,
but I was only twelve.
I saved myself, but I couldn't save her,
or could I? That question haunts me
as I ruminate on my past actions, on my fate,
which is to wait for my sister's abductor
again and again
to say, "Take me too,"
and pray, "Hail Mary, full of grace,"
before I suffocate.
Bob taps my shoulder and whispers,

"We got him."
I only nod and return to my rumination,
but he doesn't leave.
He kneels beside me
and I feel something emanating from him.
It coils and uncoils around my heart
like a snake.
I stare at him
and he asks, "What's the matter?
What's going on with you?"
I say nothing, but I'm lying.
I have "seen" something
in between Bob's conscious and unconscious
and it's mean and hard as a black diamond
as anything I've ever encountered
on my latest quest for forgiveness.
"What do you see?" he asks again.
"Nothing. . . . Nothing," I lie once more,
then I say, "What happened to you
when you were a child?"
"I was never a child," he answers cryptically.
"I live for now. That's how I make it.
You should too, but you won't.
It's got you by the throat."
"Not it," I say at last, "he has."

THE PSYCHIC DETECTIVE: INFINITY

"I'm packing it in, Bob," I say,
"I'm tired of 'seeing' things,"
but he just laughs and runs gloved hands
over the slash marks on the body
he is studying to find a pattern
by reading the cuts made
when the perp attacked with a hatchet
and pure malice.
"I don't want to interrupt your tête-à-tête,
but this was jammed inside her," says the coroner.
It is a page from the Brothers Grimm."
"Whoo-who a clue," I say, but I already knew
this killer's into fairy tales,
because he thinks reality has failed him.
"You'll never guess what else I found," he adds,
bending down and looking inside her.
Suddenly, I feel embarrassed and turn away,
then turn back and say, "It's round and metal
and when you shake it, it rattles."
"You *are* good," he says, removing the object.
"Do you think he made her insert it,
or did he do it himself, after he killed her?" he asks.
Before, I think, after he took it from his mouth. I add.

"His mouth?"
"He did it to fill her with his hatred, not just to kill her,
but to humiliate her first,
then as if quenching a thirst, drank in her hurt."
"See all the blood," adds Bob,
"the contusions? . . . Maybe he beat her with a belt, or—"
"Maybe his fist," says the coroner, sighing
and removing his gloves,
as he prepares to turn his attention elsewhere.
"Lunch?" he asks,
as if we could eat now and we decline
as we begin to define this killer by his actions.
"First one?" Bob asks.
I nod and say, "He's been thinking about it a long time,
then he snapped."
"In other words, the usual occurred."
In the parking lot, Bob says, "No semen because—"
"—Because this guy's not an ejaculator,
at least not in the body of his victim
and not on her either."
"Maybe he's impotent, or uses an article of
  clothing," says Bob
and I tell him I'm beginning to think
these killers are really demons,
but he says, "They're all too human. You know—"
"—Because I've got second sight
which more and more means I can't see
what is right in front of me,
like the reason you are looking at me funny," I say,
"I mean funnier than usual.
There's blood in your eye, dare I say it?

It's my fault for noticing things. I can't help it.
The feeling that tells me you have something to hide
is stronger than ever.
"What is it, Bob?" I ask.
"You drive this time," he says
then out of nowhere, he tells me,
"Leave it alone."
"What?"
"You know," he tells me,
getting in the driver's side after all.
"He's underground," I say.
"A basement?" Bob asks.
"Too obvious."
"A tunnel," we say in unison.
When we find the murder scene,
we get more than we bargained for,
because we discover the body of a man,
clutching a book of fairy tales in his right hand
and a gun in the other.
"Blew his brains out, oh brother," says Bob,
"another narrow escape from justice."
"If you say so," I tell him, but I don't know.
"He could be burning in hellfire now." I say.
"I wish I could be sure."
"Just assume," says Bob, "you'll sleep better if you do."
"I don't sleep you know that. Neither do you."
"For different reasons," he says.
"Whatever you say," I tell him, stepping out of the way
of the coroner, who's just arrived.
He's pissed because it's almost five
and he's got tickets to a concert.

He's taking his neglected wife, he tells us
and that we owe him.
We say we know, then wrap up and go.
Bob's off to the Bahamas for the weekend
and I'm thinking I will see some movies,
if I can handle
the violence on-screen,
but Bob asks me
how I can do my job since I'm so squeamish
and I say it's different,
but I don't know how, then I say
"Don't let what happened to your mother
ruin your good time."
He looks as if he wants to hit me,
but starts the car instead.
"When I was fourteen my father killed her,
after he raped her in front of me.
Satisfied now?" he asks.
I don't answer. I can't, because I might tell him
I know what else happened.
No, I'll just let that pass into the ether
like the victims who to us are neither alive, nor dead,
just in transit forever,
but Bob says, "You know, don't you?
A murder-suicide was really two murders,
but one of them was in self-defense."
I just tell him I can't see anything.
"Liar," he says, "you know what it feels like
to lose someone to violence.
It's what makes you sensitive."
"Maybe," I say, as my cellphone rings

and I hear about the terrible things
that happened to a five-year-old girl.
"We're on it," I say, signaling to Bob.
"Better unpack your toothbrush," I tell him
and it feels good to avoid the truth
if only for a few hours.
"The two of us are something," he says
and I answer, "We're as warped as they are."
"We aren't," he says,
"we only want to be forgiven for our sins.
Instead we end up hiding them
among the crimes others have committed."
"I've heard your pet theories before.
They're nothing more than excuses you make,
because you can't admit that you're addicted
to solving crimes, or trying to.
We're both hooked on mutilation, strangulation,
  decapitation,
should I go on? . . . I've heard this before too.
Whatever happened stays in your past.
I never asked to know your secrets, Bob,
the last one spooked me is all,
made me want to erase my memories
and replace them with scenes
straight out of greeting cards.
Instead, I see a boy
about to shoot his father through the heart."
"That's why we're partners," says Bob.
"We understand how a lucky shot
can set you free."
"Or imprison you for eternity," I tell him,

"but that's just me being optimistic."
"Come on cowboy, let's ride
and forget your toy pistol
you won't have to shoot anybody this time," I say,
as the car peels out of the lot at such high speed,
it rises off the street and we fly
like the body of a girl
hurled from an apartment building
into the murderous air.